I0476396

The Killer Instinct: Creating the Mindset to Achieve Your Maximum Potential

By Ted Dawson

TABLE OF CONTENTS

TABLE OF CONTENTS..II

CHAPTER 1 — INTRODUCING MINDSETS 1

Are People Really Different?......................................2

The Dilemma of Two Mindsets: What Does It Mean to You? 5

How Is It Possible to Turn a Failure Into a Gift? 7

CHAPTER 2 — THE TRUTH ABOUT ABILITIES AND ACCOMPLISHMENTS...12

What is the Truth?..13

1. Is Everyone Created Equal?.................................15

2. Can Everyone Do Well?..17

CHAPTER 3 — SUCCESS VS. FAILURE.......................19

What is a Failure?..22

How to be Truly Successful? 25

CHAPTER 4 — THE ABUNDANCE MINDSET: HOW TO CREATE IT?...29

What is The Abundance Mindset?............................29

How to Adopt the Abundance Mindset? 32

1. Are you short on time?...33

2. Are you short on cash? 33

3. Do you not feel loved enough?............................34

4. Are you lacking self-belief and need a boost?....35

Break the Mental Barriers..36

CHAPTER 5 — ACCEPTING RESPONSIBILITY 38

Only You Are Responsible for Your Fate 38

How to Start Accepting Responsibility in Life?..... 43

Blame vs. Accepting Responsibility 47

CHAPTER 6 — ACCEPTING AND AVOIDING CRITICISM 50

Filtering Criticism — How to Differentiate Between Positive and Negative Criticism 51

How to Avoid Negative Criticism and Accept Positive Criticism?... 54

CHAPTER 7 — 12 TIPS TO HELP YOU ACHIEVE YOUR MAXIMUM POTENTIAL 57

1. Evaluate Your Life.. 57

2. Become an Optimist 58

3. Rid Yourself of Excuses 59

4. Don't Sell Yourself Short....................................... 61

5. Start Learning... 62

6. Be Grateful.. 64

7. Accept Change 64

8. Plan Ahead and Focus on Long Term Planning 66

9. Become Mentally Strong 68

10. Set Shorter Goals... 69

11. Take Action... 71

12. Become Your Own Competition......................... 71

CHAPTER 1 — INTRODUCING MINDSETS

Have you ever wondered why people are so different from each other?

Let me rephrase my question. Have you ever wondered why people act so differently from each other in a given situation?

Some people act bravely. They are not afraid of whatever it is coming. They don't hide themselves waiting for it to be over. Instead, they jump right into it. Those people take risks and try to leverage that position for their benefits and rewards. In the end, most often than not, that risk pays off.

On the other hand, in a similar situation, some people will act defensively. They prefer not to risk anything. Instead, they try to minimize their losses. This second group of people is not interested in leveraging a given situation for their benefits. Instead, they are more focused on defending —

rather than expanding — what belongs to them.

So why is that?

Why do people act differently when they all are exposed to a somewhat similar situation?

The answer lies in the study of "mindsets".

Are People Really Different?

You see, people are not exactly different. It is their different mindsets that set them apart and encourage them to take a certain path while others avoid it.

This topic — whether people are really different from each other or not — has been a matter of debate for far too long. Experts from both sides have lined up their claims.

One such group of experts claimed that difference is inevitable and that it stems from various physical, emotional, and hereditary differences. This group believed that you can't fight the differences of people. It is automatic and completely natural. Some of them even claimed that the alleged physical differences — for example, the bumps on the skull, the size and shape of the skull and genes — play the most important role in people's different behaviors.

2

Similarly, many experts believed that the differences in a person's background, training levels, learning processes, and life experiences, contribute to that. You will be surprised to know that Alfred Binet, the famous creator of the IQ test, was also of the same view. Moreover, the IQ test was never, in fact, designed, to summarize a kid's unchangeable intelligence level. As a matter of fact, Alfred Binet strongly believed that although different children have different intelligence levels, with thorough learning processes, the intelligence level and capabilities of children could be increased.

In one of his famous books, Modern Ideas about Children, he said:

"A few modern philosophers ... assert that an individual's intelligence is a fixed quantity, a quantity that cannot be increased. We must protest and react against this brutal pessimism. With practice, training, and, above all, method, we manage to increase our attention, our memory, our judgment and literally to become more intelligent than we were before."

As you can see, intelligence does not always have to be in a predefined and fixed quantity.

And as this book is all about achieving your maximum potential, it must give you great comfort in knowing that you can increase your abilities and level of intelligence.

But how does a person do that?

Moreover, if we do not have a predefined and fixed quantity of intelligence, why do certain people seem more capable, active and intelligent than others? What is the main reason then — if not a fixed level of intelligence — that makes two people different from each other? What is it that one makes a person a failure while it makes another person an astonishing success?

Again, the answer is the different mindsets of those two people.

The person, who is getting successful, unlocking new potentials, exploring new opportunities, making money, generating buzz, and getting a lot of attention, has a very positive mindset. He has the kind of mindset that propels him to move forward in life, accept challenges, accept and avoid negative criticisms, and help him grow.

The other person has a negative mindset that does not allow him to be either aggressive or successful.

He always lives in fear, and he does not have the courage to follow his dreams. More importantly, he can't see opportunities, he can't let go of his mistakes, and he can't perform tasks efficiently and effectively.

The Dilemma of Two Mindsets: What Does It Mean to You?

It is all good when you read about it. But the bottom line is that what does all of it mean for you?

Understanding the difference of these two mindsets can lead you to so many good things in life. It forms the very basis of this book and how you can — by adopting a better mindset — achieve your maximum potential. So pay a lot of attention to this section, and you will have almost half of your job done.

Do you remember the famous quote that says: "A man becomes what he thinks of himself."

It is true. The view you adopt for yourself greatly affects the way you lead your life. It can either determine whether you are going to become a very successful person or fail miserably. This view decides whether you successfully accomplish all the things you ever wanted to and become the person you always wanted to become or not.

Most people do not believe this. They wonder how a simple psychological belief can affect and alter your life so much. Let me explain how does it affect and then you can decide whether it is affecting you, too.

You see, first of all, there is this fixed mindset. It makes you believe that all your qualities are fixed and permanently carved in stone. It makes you believe that you cannot change your traits or qualities and, therefore, it requires you to prove yourself constantly over and over.

A major portion of this mindset is created in our childhood. This is a stage when we are led to believe that a person's IQ scores tell the whole story of who they are and how intelligent they can be. Only the highest IQ kids would be able to participate in various high-end school activities. This judgmental stance makes us more focused on always being the smartest one and, ultimately, leads to our fixed mindsets.

This is what you spend most of your time wondering:

- Will I fail or succeed?

- Will I be accepted or rejected?

- Will I feel smart or stupid?

- Will I be the winner or loser?

How Is It Possible to Turn a Failure Into a Gift?

When you are being taught to have a fixed mindset for your entire life, it can be really difficult to come instantly out of it. It takes a lot of practice, commitment, persistence and positive attitude to overcome this menace of fixed mindset that is not allowing you to grow and be successful.

The only solution is to turn your failures into a gift and your fixed mindset into a growth and more positive mindset.

Imagine the following scenario.

You are suddenly a young adult who is studying a university. You wake up one morning, get into your car and start driving to the university. On the road, you get a road ticket. Already frustrated, you get to the class — a class you particularly like and pretty good at. Your teacher hands you over the mid-term papers and you see that you have got a C in your exams. On the way back to your home, you get a really bad phone call that completely pisses you off.

What would you do and feel in such a situation?

The most common responses of a fixed mindset person would be:

- I'm a complete failure

- Why is my life so hard and difficult?

- I am the unluckiest person in this whole world.

- Nobody loves me.

- Everything bad only happens to me.

- Why me?!

These are the most feelings in these scenarios, but let me ask you a question. Are these feelings and reactions completely justified?

It was just a bad result and a bad phone call. Nobody died, at least.

The above reactions indicate that you are not coping with failure, while you should be transforming this failure into a gift.

You need to take these bad events — these failures — and see them as new opportunities to improve yourself, to get better results and, most importantly, to achieve your maximum potential.

A person with a better mindset does not react the same way as a fixed mindset person would do. Even in difficult times likes these, people with better mindset are always optimistic, positive and looking to the future. Unlike the fixed mindset people, who feel completely paralyzed and an utter failure after such events, the growth mindset population always finds a way to deal with bad situations.

If the exact same situation happened to a person with the growth mindset, some of the most common reactions would be:

- Thank the God that it is only a C, and not an F.

- Phew! Good thing that it was only a road ticket and not a car wreck.

- I'm glad that my C didn't come in my final exams. I now know that I have some work to do in order to improve myself.
- I can now be better with my communications since that last bad phone call.
- It was just a bad phone call. At least I didn't get completely rejected by a friend.
- I will study harder from now on, and I'll make sure that I don't get a bad result anymore.

Sometimes, situations can be really difficult to deal with. But we all get through them eventually, right?

It is not like that the growth mindset people enjoy being in difficult situations or the fact that they just don't care. That would be wrong. The only difference is that when exposed to difficult scenarios, people with a better mindset do not throw their hands up, blame themselves, get depressed, or run away. They summon the courage to confront the challenges, fight the difficult scenarios, identify the real problem, and find practical ways to deal with it.

By now you have learned the basics of fixed mindset and growth mindset, the major differences between the two. Moreover, you have also learned some of the negative impacts of the fixed mindset and the positive impacts of the growth mindset. Now we are going to discuss another really important concept in our very next chapter of this book.

It is about your fictional mental barrier that does not allow you to match the standards of other successful people.

The question is: "Are you capable enough?"

CHAPTER 2 — THE TRUTH ABOUT ABILITIES AND ACCOMPLISHMENTS

More often than not, it is the mystified truth about abilities and accomplishments that does not allow you to grow and become successful.

You get intimidated by success stories of other people — instead of being motivated. Your mind suddenly takes the backseat, becomes defensive, and make you believe that, "You can't do that. You are not capable enough."

When you refer to that other person who successfully achieved what he wanted to achieve, your mind presents another excuse, "Well, don't talk about him. He was privileged. He had a lot of opportunities and luxuries, so he did it. And just because he did doesn't mean you can do it, too. Look at yourself!"

Do not pay any attention to it. There are a lot of things about abilities and accomplishments that I am sure you do not know.

So let's discuss the truth about abilities and

accomplishments.

What is the Truth?

Try to imagine Thomas Edison as vividly as you possibly can. Now, tell me what is he doing and where is he? Is he alone? Is he working?

Most people would imagine and say, "Yes, he is alone, and he is working in his workshop. He is trying to invent new things."

Most of the people imagine him working alone because they believe Edison was the only one who knew what he was after. However, the reality reveals a very different picture.

As a matter of fact, several records show that Edison wasn't a loner at all. He had around 30 assistants and well-trained scientists in a very start of the art laboratory. Moreover, the invention of light bulb that became a great single moment in Edison's life didn't happen instantly. There was months of work behind that one moment and a whole lot of time-consuming activities and smaller innovations from many different mathematicians, physicists, chemists, and engineers.

The biographer of Thomas Edison, Paul Israel, reveals that Thomas Edison was more or less a very regular boy of his place, time, and era. And the only thing that set him apart from the others was his mindset and drive. He was always curious, trying to find new things, without being bogged down.

His famous quote tells a lot about his commitment, perseverance and positive attitude:

"I have not failed 10,000 times. I have just found 10,000 ways that do not work."

So what did you learn from this example?

The lesson to be learned is that the truth behind "geniuses" and "extraordinary people" is a rather simple one. They worked hard, worked consistently, and stayed positive till the very end — even, and especially, when others failed, lost hope and stopped working.

The truth about abilities is that everybody has certain abilities that they can put into good use. And anybody can get those achievements and accomplishments if they stay in it for long enough, and with a positive frame of mind.

So, assuming what I just said is true, a common mind

asks two important questions.

Does it mean that:

- Is everyone created equal?

- Can everyone do well?

Let's try to answer these questions with the help of metaphors and examples. The answer to these two questions will help you find the real truth of abilities and accomplishments, and how you can use that to unlock your own true potential.

I am going to start with the first question.

1. Is Everyone Created Equal?

In a nutshell, no.

There are a few people who are just "born genius". You know, the kind of little kids who do amazing and extraordinary things that kids their age can't even think of?

So first things first, there are a few people in this world who are just born with "gifts". They have heightened intelligence levels, abilities, and interests. Using those gifts, they eventually achieve great things.

Let me give you an example.

Michael was a young kid who was a true genius. Even when he was a little kid, he used to play games that involved numbers and letters. He used to ask dozens of questions to his parents, as he had obsessive interests and a lot of curiosities.

The most amazing thing about Michael was that he started playing, reading, speaking, and doing mathematics at a very young age. In fact, and whether you believe it or not, at just five months old, Michael could ask, "What's for dinner?"

By the age of three, he became quite proficient with algebra. He was not only solving algebraic equations, but he was also proving algebraic formulas and discovering new algebraic rules.

He had an innate amazing ability. But given said that, Michael's most interesting feature and ability was to stay focused and curious about the things he loved. It must have taken a lot of efforts for such a young kid to skip playing games, watching cartoons, or playing outside, and instead doing algebraic equations. But he did, and that's what made him special. In short, he had the mindset for it.

So, generally speaking, is it the ability or the

mindset?

Was Mozart — the famous musician — was just really capable or it was the fact that he used to work really hard — so much so that his hands eventually become deformed?

Similarly, was it Darwin's innate scientific ability that made him famous or was it the fact that he started collecting specimens nonstop from a relatively early age.

How did they achieve those things: via their abilities or mindset?

I hope you get the point. It's the mindset, dedication, and a positive attitude.

Now, let's answer the second question.

2. Can Everyone Do Well?

If this is true that it was mainly their mindsets and not just their abilities to achieve something so spectacular, then comes the more important question:

Can everyone do well?

The truth is that, yes, everyone can do well in his or

her own life. Whether you believe in yourself or not, there are certain abilities in everybody. And by using those abilities, you can achieve and accomplish things that you always wanted to.

The question should not be:

"Can I do it?"

Instead, it should be:

"What is the best way that I can do it?"

CHAPTER 3 — SUCCESS VS. FAILURE

If you really want to achieve your maximum potential in life, then this is one of the most important chapters you will ever read.

What is a success? What is a failure? And how do you differentiate between the two? This understanding is the key to your success.

What is a Success?

People who have growth mindset find success in doing their best. They are not overly obsessed with proving anything. They are not particularly crazy about winning or losing. It is their will to compete with their own self that makes them superior to others.

For instance, Jackie Joyner-Kersee tells us that, "For me the joy of athletics has never resided in winning. I derive just as much happiness from the process as from the results. I don't mind losing as long as I see improvement, or I feel I have done as well as I possibly could. If I lose, I just go back to the work and work some more."

The idea is that personal success is only achieved when you work your hardest to become your best version. It isn't about winning or losing as long as you're improving yourself and becoming the best version you could be. This was also the motto of John wooden's life. He said:

"There were many, many games that gave me as much pleasure as any of the ten national championship games we won, simply because we prepared fully and played near our highest level of ability."

Another example is that of the great Tiger Woods. He was one of the fiercest competitors who ever lived. He used to love winning, but what counted most for Tiger Woods was the effort he made even when he couldn't win. He could actually be proud of his efforts.

For instance, Tiger Woods was really disappointed that he did not win the 98' Masters tournament. But he still managed to feel good about his top 10 finish. He said, "I squeezed the towel dry this week. I am very proud of the way I hung in there."

After a British open where he finished third, he said,

"Sometimes you get even more satisfaction out of creating a score when things aren't completely perfect, when you're not feeling so well about your swing."

And do notice that we are not talking about an unambitious person. Tiger Woods was a hugely ambitious man. And as I mentioned earlier, he did not like losing. He always strived hard to become the best.

These are the qualities of a person with the growth mindset. On the contrary, people with fixed mindsets do not value efforts and hard-work as much as they ideally should. In fact, they are often only obsessed with winning and not losing.

For them, success is all about establishing their dominance and superiority over others. However, this could not be any more wrong. This stems from the wrong fixed mindset that does not allow people to look beyond their personal achievements — however limited and small they may be. Fixed mindsets make people see only what is in front of them. It does not allow you to become a visionary, explore hidden opportunities, and unlock your maximum potential.

What is a Failure?

What is a failure for people with a bad mindset as well as for people who have a growth mindset?

People, who have better and positive mindsets, find motivation and inspiration in setbacks and failures. They consider those failures only as temporary setbacks and do not allow such difficult situations to break them completely. They honestly believe that failures and temporary setbacks are wake-up calls and it's not the end of the world if they don't always succeed in the very first attempt.

Instead, when they face setbacks and failures, they try to learn from them, and then work on their weaknesses, only to come back stronger as ever.

Let me give you a very inspiring example.

Kareem Abdul-Jabbar, who was an excellent basketball player, had a signature shot — the dunk. The college basketball outlawed his signature shot. Most people thought that it was the end of Kareem's career and that he would never reach the top again.

But Kareem did not have a fixed mindset. He took inspiration from that temporary setback and did not allow it to take control of him.

He did not start whining. Instead, he worked thrice as hard as he used to do and developed many other shots.

Some of the famous shots he later developed are:

- Kareem's famous bank shot off the glass.

- Skyhook

- The turnaround jumper.

He did not let the setback label him. Instead, he worked hard, took control and overcame the difficult situation.

But, on the other hand, negative people with fixed mindsets take these temporary setbacks as permanent failures. They believe that they will never be able to do it again, even without trying the second time. They let the setbacks label them, define them, and dictate their whole lives.

The main problem with people having fixed mindsets is that they are very rigid in their beliefs, thinking, and approaches. They either think that they are the king of the world and anything they do will always be perfect or they believe the complete opposite of it that they can't do anything right.

Let me give you an example of Sergio Garcia, who rocked the golf world when he first came onto the scene. Many embraced Garcia as the next Tiger Woods.

He had some excellent shots in his armory, and he performed really well when he was riding high with confidence. However, when his form dipped, his charm, confidence, and belief did, too.

Since he had a fixed mindset instead of the growth mindset, he became obsessed with his failures. Instead of finding the real problem and working harder, he started firing caddie after caddie, blaming them for his poor performance and everything that was happening at that stage. Moreover, he once blamed his shoe when he could not take a shot and instead slipped.

You can easily see the difference between the two different types of people. So which one are you?

To summarize until now, understand that:

True success is becoming the best version of yourself. It is to upgrade yourself, acquire new knowledge, practice harder, and perform the best you could. It is definitely not about winning or losing, or proving your dominance over others.

Similarly, failure is only a temporary setback. It does not define you, your career, your relationships, or your life. It is just a part of an overall large process that is bound to happen at some stage. Don't let failures or temporary setbacks label you. Instead, find the root cause of the problem, accept responsibilities, and start working harder. And when you fail, remember that even Einstein failed in his life.

How to be Truly Successful?

If you have understood the real meaning of true success and failure, it is time to start implementing those advices in your life.

The question is rather simple: How to be truly successful in your life?

The answer, apparently, isn't — at least for the fixed mindset people. However, for people with a positive attitude or the growth mindset — or even for the people like you, who are currently reading this book — success is a very simple concept.

The idea is that you have to take charge of the processes that bring success in your life. Once you manage to do it, all you have to do is to maintain it and you will enjoy success after success.

For example, how do you think Michael Jordan stayed one of the best basketball players even when he was getting older. He lost a lot of stamina, agility and reflexes with age, but was it enough to stop him? Definitely not!

Why? Because he took charge of the processes that were going to make him successful. When he realized that he no longer has the agility and stamina he once used to have, he started compensating on other departments. For instance, he worked even harder on conditioning and on his moves, e.g., his celebrated fallaway jumper and the turnaround jump shot.

If you can remember, you will realize that he came into the league as a slam-dunker, but he left as one of the most complete players ever to play the game.

Just like Michael Jordan, Tiger Woods also managed his motivation and used it to his own success.

To understand what he did and how he did it, first understand that golf is a tough and unpredictable game. According to the famous coach, Butch Harmon, "The golf swing is just about the farthest thing from a perfectible discipline in athletics. The most reliable swings are only relatively repeatable. They never stop being works in progress. That's why even the biggest golf star wins only a fraction of a time and may not win for long periods of time."

Tiger's dad knew this. So he made sure to sharpen Tiger's attention level and course strategy. He used to make very loud noises or throw things at Tiger Wood just when he was about to make this shot. In short, he prepared him for distractions that were bound to come later in his life.

Similarly, when Tiger Woods was just three years old, his father was already teaching him about course management. Now, Tiger is so proficient that he constantly experiments with what works best and what doesn't, but he is never distracted from the long-term game plan he always has in place.

In his own words, "I know my game. I know what I want to achieve, and I know how to get there."

More importantly, instead of becoming self-obsessed with winning or losing, Woods enjoy the process. He says, "I love working on shots, carving them this way and that and proving to myself that I can hit a certain shot on command."

If you want to be truly successful, you will need to have a similar approach and mindset like this. You can't hide away from the problems and hope to conceal them with something else — just as people with the fixed mindsets do.

For instance, John McEnroe, who had a fixed mindset, used to hide behind excuses and lame justifications whenever he faced tough situations. His primary focus was always on concealing his flaws, instead of accepting them and improving himself. Perhaps, this is why instead of fixing his problems, he wished that he played a team sport. In his own words, "If you are not at your peak, you can hide it so much easier in a team sport."

You can easily identify a very negative mindset here. Instead of improving and working harder, a sportsman openly concealed his flaws and wished he played a different game. How could he achieve his maximum potential with this kind of mindset and attitude? Neither can you.

Remember that the next time you face a failure — or a temporary setback as we like to call it.

CHAPTER 4 — THE ABUNDANCE MINDSET: HOW TO CREATE IT?

By now, we have already discussed a lot of differences and importance aspects of the growth mindset and the fixed mindset. We are certainly going to discuss more about them as they are really important for you if you are going to achieve your maximum potential.

But in this chapter, let's take a look at another very important concept, i.e., The Abundance Mindset.

Let's start with the basics first.

What is The Abundance Mindset?

The abundance mindset is actually very simple: give away what you got.

It's not that complicated really; it has a very simple concept, but most people struggle with it.

Imagine what most people would do if they stumble upon a great idea?

Yes, you guessed it right. They would hoard that idea

and never let it go. They protect that idea with all their might and make sure no one is ever able to reach it.

What are they afraid of? What are they living in fear that someone else will come and take that idea away from them? They always end up thinking that they should save that particular idea for later.

This is thinking approach of a pure pessimist. If you are holding on to an idea, thinking that someone will take it away from you, you are implying that you are only going to stumble on one good idea in your entire life. Isn't it right?

This is the same approach of living in fear that does not let you grow or help you achieve your maximum potential.

However, you should be more positive, thinking that you are going to have lots of great ideas in your life — because you are worthy enough.

Let's have a look at "bloggers". In this scenario, they are the perfect example for us.

What do bloggers basically do? How do they earn money? How do they develop their fan following?

And no, I'm not talking about those bloggers who

just share their opinions and personal life experiences. I'm talking about professional bloggers who work within a certain niche or industry, and have a very clear business model.

Regardless, bloggers basically earn their rep and fan following by providing lots of free, exclusive and valuable information to their readers. They give valuable ideas to their blog readers and help them grow on a personal and professional level.

But what would happen to a blogger who stops sharing that information and valuable ideas with his / her readers? People would stop reading that blog and it will fail very soon.

You see, the whole concept is to give away what you have and not hoard those ideas in fear. And believe me or not, it is no different from money.

"But I don't have enough money to spend. That's why I save." It is one of the most common responses whenever you ask someone why they are always holding money, only never to spend it.

However, it's not the truth. As a matter of fact, they don't spend because they are afraid that they might never be able to earn that money back. This is where the fixed and negative mindset kicks in, defeating the better growth and abundance mindset.

It always keeps you in tension and frustration.

How to Adopt the Abundance Mindset?

People are always short on important things. It does not matter if it is time, ideas, money, or love, most people believe that they just don't have enough. This is often the root cause of all problems.

If you are not ready to give, you will never be ready to receive.

Brad Jensen puts it beautifully in the following words:

"You receive through the same doorway through which you give. The way to receive freely is to give freely. Quality is more important than quantity since the universe amplifies thought into circumstance. Begin giving and let God perfect your giving."

Following are a few really important tips to help you lead on the path of The Abundance Mindset.

1. Are you short on time?

If you are short on time — like most people are — it is time to let yourself go. Do not try to do more things in a lesser amount of time. Instead, start giving your time to other people. Specifically put aside some time to spend it with other people that you love and care about.

It does not mean that you stop doing your work and start spending 90% of your time with others. That would be unproductive. The key is to find a proper balance between spending time with others and doing your things — a balance between giving and receiving.

Volunteering for a good cause is an excellent way to get started.

2. Are you short on cash?

Most of the people who do not spend enough say that they are short on cash. While some of them would genuinely be short on cash, it is not always the case for the majority of people.

Here is a weird advice.

If you are short on cash, consider giving some of it away to other people. Do a bit of charity or give some cash to your friends in need. What matters the most is that you feel good and positive about yourself. And most importantly, you become fearless of the thought of not having enough money.

This is a mental barrier that always stops you from growing, improving and unlocking your maximum potential. If you never spend money and keep holding on to your savings, you will never be able to earn more than you are currently earning. You will have enough, and there will be a lot less motivation to achieve the extraordinary.

3. Do you not feel loved enough?

It is also a very common scenario, right? A lot of the people fail and stay depressed because they think that they are not loved enough.

If that is the case with you, go out, reach out to people who you love and care about and give free hugs to at least five such people.

Giving always leads to receiving. You will be a lot happier after you are done with the hugs. You will even notice a few people who will hug you back, making you feel loved again. You will start loving your life, and suddenly things will become a lot clearer that it isn't so bad out there.

It is important to understand that only when you are 100% satisfied with your life and everything in it, you can grab opportunities, achieve your maximum potential, and become the best version of yourself. A distracted and depressed mind does not allow you to achieve those levels of excellence.

4. Are you lacking self-belief and need a boost?

This happens more often than you'd like to admit, right?

I mean, it happens to everybody. So it isn't like there is something wrong with you.

If you lack self-belief and if there are doubts about your confidence, it is time to heal someone else. You will automatically find a way to your own problems.

Spend some time with a person who is in a similar situation like yours. If one of your friends is lacking confidence and self-belief, make it your job to help him get back on his feet. Console your friend and tell him that everything is going to be all right.

Once you do it — and once you seriously mean it — you realize that everything is going to be all right for you, too.

Fill their minds with positive attitudes and ideas. Tell them how awesome they are, and how you are damn sure that they are going to make it. Tell your friends that you are proud of them and that they should not lose hope.

It's magical how when you start believing in someone else's abilities and traits, you start believing yourself, too.

Break the Mental Barriers

The key is to break the fictional mental barriers that are not even there. It's only in your mind, and when you start believing in yourself, all those doubts go away.

And the best way of breaking those mental barriers is by adopting a very positive, giving mindset, i.e., The Abundance Mindset.

Everybody is in a different sort of situation. So do not

worry if you can't give some of the things I mentioned above. You might have something different to give away — it is often the thing you want the most from other people.

- If you lack belief in yourself, start believing others.

- If you need people to trust you, start trusting others.

- If you are stuck in someplace, help someone.

- If you have run out of ideas, give advices to someone in need of them.

- If you don't feel loved enough, start loving others.

And all of it will come back to you in due time, and you will be able to achieve a lot of new things that you could not have ever imagined.

CHAPTER 5 — ACCEPTING RESPONSIBILITY

Let me ask you a simple question.

When something goes wrong, what do you do?

Do you blame someone — or something — else or you do accept full responsibility of it, even if you think someone else did it to you?

This is important because this is exactly what defines your personality, your growth level, and your overall potential.

In this chapter, we are going to discuss a whole lot of important things about "accepting responsibility". If you truly get what this chapter is trying to teach you, you will definitely become a lot better version of yourself.

So let's get started.

Only You Are Responsible for Your Fate

Once you understand this really simple concept, life

becomes a lot simpler and easier for you.

Simply put, only you are responsible for whatever happens to you — good or bad. There is simply no one else who could benefit you or harm you if you do not want it.

There is a very famous quote by Mr. Henry Ford that perfectly describes this situation. He says:

"Whether you think you can or you think you can't — you are right."

What does this tell you? It tells you — very specifically — that whatever happens to you or whatever it is that you are going to achieve is only limited by your mindset, approach, and the steps you take to accomplish it.

If you fail in an exam, you can either blame your life, your neighborhood, the distractions that were around you, your family problems, the monetary problems you might be facing or anything else. Or, on the other hand, you can buckle up, put your hands up, and admit that you just weren't good enough this time, and now you are going to work even harder to improve the results next time.

The primary issue with not accepting responsibility is

that you do not identify the main problem and the reason why it happened. And you can't solve what you can't find.

You must have heard it a thousand times: acceptance is the first step towards success. In this scenario, accepting your responsibility is going to be the very first step towards becoming a better version of yourself (the growth mindset accomplishment goal) and maximizing your true potential.

Let's compare two different groups of people, what they say, and how they behave in similar situations.

The first group accepts responsibility, understands the gravity of the situation, and strive to work harder and become better. You want to belong to this group.

The second group of people is the one that does not accept responsibility in any case whatsoever. Those are the people who unnecessarily blame other external factors, without identifying the real cause of the issue.

Let's see some of the common responses of each of these groups. If you are not sure which group do you belong to, take a hint.

- People who accept their responsibilities usually have the following responses:

- They truly acknowledge that they are solely responsible for their choices and actions in life.

- They understand that only they choose the direction of their lives.

- They are mature enough to realize that they can't blame others for the choices they make.

- They know they have complete control over what to think, feel, or choose.

- They identify negative feelings, hostility, anger, pessimism, and depression and work against them.

- They say, "I'm going to work harder from now on."

On the other hand, people who fail to accept responsibility have a very negative and unrealistic outlook on life. They are overly dependent on others for recognition, approval, acceptance, or affection.

Perhaps this is the main reason why they blame others, and not themselves, for anything that goes wrong in their lives. They are emotionally and physically unhealthy, often unsuccessful in personal relationships, fearful of taking risks, grabbing opportunities, accepting changes, or making a decision. All of which ultimately leads to them not being able to achieve their maximum potential.

Following are a few responses you commonly hear from people who do not accept responsibility in their lives:

- It's not my fault.

- Life is unfair.

- God has asked too much of me this time.

- How can I handle it? It is impossible.

- I just want to kill myself.

- Nobody loves me.

- How can you say that I'm responsible for what happens to me in my future?

- I cannot make my own destiny. It is all about luck and fortune.

- Some people are just born lucky. I am not one of them.

- Life is always so depressing.

- Somebody help me.

- This all happened because of him / her.

- Hard work is not the answer. It does not matter how hard I work; I am never going to get ahead and become successful.

- I am who I am. I should not be changed, and no one should ask me to change myself.

With this kind of an attitude, nothing improves.

How to Start Accepting Responsibility in Life?

The moment when you can start accepting responsibility in life, everything will start falling into the right places.

You will feel better, think better, and you will be grabbing new opportunities in life that you never thought was possible. Most importantly, you will start becoming the best version of yourself that you can ever become, and it will maximize your true potential.

In this section, I am going to list down a few behavioral changes, tips, and tricks that you will have to adopt, in order to be more responsible and to stay away from the futile blame-game.

Some of the changes that you will have to make in your lifestyle are:

➢ First of all, accept that you are not at your best and that you do not take responsibility of your actions and choices. Acceptance is always the first step.

➢ Seek out and accept help wherever and whenever you find it.

➢ Adopt the abundance mindset.

➢ Ditch the fixed mindset and start adapting the growth mindset instead.

➢ Be more positive. Do not let negative thoughts cloud over your mind.

- Start trusting people.

- Be open and more acceptable to new ideas. Most opportunities come from new ideas.

- Accept that change isn't always bad. More often than not, changes can be good.

- Become more responsive to changes. Design your life in a way that you can be more responsive to what is going to come your way next.

- Let go of anger, blame, fear, insecurities, and mistrust.

- Make new friends and keep contact with the old ones.

- Start exercising. You should realize that only you are responsible for your own health. If you do not pay attention to your own health, you can't do it for anything else either.

- Recognize and reorganize your priorities and goals.

- Accept that other people may help you here and there, but you should not be solely dependent on them.
- Stop making excuses. A person who really wants to do something finds a way, while others find excuses.
- Live your life by this simple rule: "When there is a will, there is a way."
- Overcome fears.
- Take more calculated risks. Only you can propel yourself up and towards success.
- Realize and identify your strengths and use them.
- Also, identify your weaknesses and start improving on those areas.

It is never easy to flip your life altogether. But as you must have realized, it is extremely important to start moving in the right direction.

There is one more thing to learn before we end this chapter. It is an important concept, so pay a lot of attention.

Blame vs. Accepting Responsibility

It is always good to accept the responsibility of whatever it is that happen to you, but you will also have to be very, very careful with it. This is because it is very hard to differentiate between accepting responsibility and blaming yourself.

You see, there is a very fine line between the two. While accepting responsibility for whatever happens to you and your life, you can easily fall into the trap of blaming yourself.

Understand that the primary purpose of your life — and of this book, too — is to achieve your maximum potential. You cannot do it while you are blaming yourself for all the things that go wrong in your life. Accepting responsibility is different from blaming yourself, but the problem is that the line that differentiates the two is a thin one.

What are some of the confusing aspects of these two terms? The following section will enlighten you and help you so you can differentiate these two phenomena.

- Responsibly accepting your own interference in your life's choices and decisions is a good thing. Blaming yourself isn't.
- Accepting your responsibility in your life's decisions requires you to be practical and rational about it. Blaming yourself can be very ignorant.
- If you are not looking at the facts objectively, chances are that you are only blaming yourself for a bad thing that happened to you.
- Accepting responsibility requires you to take a look at all the facts logically. If it leads back to you, you should accept responsibility for it. Most likely, it won't be blaming yourself.
- If you are in doubt, seek professional advice.
- Ask your friends if you are responsible for a certain situation or not.
- Evaluate yourself objectively and find out if you have been lacking in a certain

department. If you have been lacking, it is
time to accept responsibility.

- Make sure to understand that you can't
  predict future events. If something bad
  happens to you — as a result of a nature's act
  — you should not blame yourself.

Remember that responsibility and accepting
responsibility for your actions is empowering. It is
not depressing or fearful. It is the ability to respond
to a certain situation in a manner you deem best.
Moreover, it is also about realizing and identifying
the areas you can improve.

However, on the other hand, blaming yourself — or
anyone else for a situation — is often the easy way
out. It is definitely not productive, and it leads to
worse situations. You cannot grow as a result of
blaming yourself. And it is absolutely impossible that
blaming yourself would even remotely help you in
achieving your maximum and true potential in life.

CHAPTER 6 — ACCEPTING AND AVOIDING CRITICISM

In order to unlock and achieve your maximum potential, you should be able to accept and avoid criticism.

But isn't it contradictory? To accept and avoid criticism? How do you do them simultaneously?

The simplest answer lies in the understanding that criticism has two different types:

Positive criticism

Negative criticism

The idea is to be able to differentiate between the two types of criticism. Then, once you have successfully identified the specific type of criticism you are receiving in a given situation, accept the positive criticism and avoid the negative one.

Filtering Criticism — How to Differentiate Between Positive and Negative Criticism

On paper, it seems rather easy. But it is definitely one of the most difficult tasks to successfully differentiate between positive and negative criticism.

When you mess up, you will find 2 types of people around you: one of the two groups would be genuinely interested in helping you recover and grow, while the second one would just make things worse.

Remember that there is a fine line between the two different types of criticism. Even positive criticism has a tendency to fall into the category of "harmful praises". And, similarly, negative criticism can often be motivating and inspiring — but it can have a long-term negative impact on your overall life.

So how do you differentiate between the two?

Following are a few tips to help you identify and differentiate between positive criticism and negative criticism:

- Positive criticism does not confine your abilities or intelligence level. But negative criticism does, and it makes you believe that you have limited abilities that are just not enough to successfully complete a given task.

- Positive criticism encourages you to get back on your feet, work harder and complete the task you started in the first place. Negative criticism, on the other hand, justifies that you can't complete that task, and it is okay to let it go.

- Negative criticism targets personalities, characters and traits of a person. Remember what we learned in the first chapter: with proper training and learning experience, every person has the capability to undertake and successfully complete any task.

- Positive criticism improves your confidence and self-belief. On the other hand, negative criticism ruins your confidence.

- Negative criticism creates a difference between you and society. It basically puts you beneath other peers, making your less worthy and less capable.

The bottom line is that whenever you come across criticism, it is important that you should be able to identify between the two different types.

If it is positive criticism, which is helping you see things clearly and practically, and helping you grow and overtake the situation with a very positive attitude and frame of mind, accept it.

Do not fight it. People, who have a fixed mindset, can't digest positive criticism, and it is one of the biggest reasons why they fail.

Remember the example of Sergio Garcia, who blamed everything for his poor performance, instead of blaming his lack of handwork and commitment to the game?

He wasn't able to digest positive criticism. He could

not accept the fact that he just wasn't trying hard enough and that he should have worked harder in order to overcome his poor form. If he could understand and accept criticism, he might have practiced harder instead of blaming every other thing.

How to Avoid Negative Criticism and Accept Positive Criticism?

There is no hard and fast rule here.

It takes time, persistence, and a lot maturity to be able to listen to criticism — let alone accepting it.

Whatever criticism comes your way, it is important to listen to it with an open mind. After listening to it as neutrally as you possible could if you still believe that it is only a negative form of criticism, just avoid it. Do not pay a lot of attention to it, trust in your abilities, and prove the other person wrong.

Similarly, also try to be positive and accepting of any positive criticism that comes to your way. Only if you are truly willing to improve, you will be able to understand and accept positive criticism. And it does help you in the long run.

There is a famous trick for avoiding criticism. It says:

"Say nothing, do nothing, and be nothing." Actually this wonderful piece of advice is adapted by a quote from Elbert Hubbard. His actual words are:

"Criticism is something you can avoid easily —

by saying nothing, by doing nothing, and by

being nothing."

You should stick to this rule for the rest of your life in order to successfully avoiding negative criticism. There will always be a few people who will throw negative criticisms and negative vibes your way, but it is your job to avoid that. And the best technique to avoiding those negative vibes is by being silent and doing what is right for you.

Here, I would like to quote Theodore Roosevelt. He said:

"It is not the critic who counts, not the man who points out how the strong man stumbled, or where the doer of deeds could have done better. The credit goes the man who is actually in the arena, whose face is marred by dust and sweat and blood, who strives valiantly, who errs and comes short and short again, who knows the great enthusiasms, the great devotions, and spends himself in a worthy cause, who at best knows achievement and who at the worst if he fails at least fails while daring greatly so that his place shall never be with those cold and timid souls who know neither victory nor defeat."

CHAPTER 7 — 12 TIPS TO HELP YOU ACHIEVE YOUR MAXIMUM POTENTIAL

The above chapters gave you a lot of idea of the mindsets you need to achieve your maximum potential.

However, having just the mindset does not guarantee you success. You also need to adapt and change your life, activities, and routines accordingly.

In this chapter, we are going to discuss 12 really helpful tips that will help you achieve your maximum potential. Some of these tips will look a bit difficult, but, believe me, they are not. With just a little bit of care, attention, and persistence, you will easily adopt the lifestyle you need.

So here are 12 tips to help you improve your lifestyle and achieve your maximum potential.

1. Evaluate Your Life

You can't fix what you do not know, right?

Therefore, the first tip is to evaluate your life and see what is wrong with it. The only way to achieve your maximum potential is first to know your limitations and the things that are not entirely perfect with your life.

After all, your primary goal is to work on your weaknesses so that you can become an overall excellent package.

Evaluating yourself does not mean you need to spend 30 minutes a day, closing your eyes and meditating. But it is a good idea to get yourself away from all the distractions and noise of a normal life and see what you need to achieve in your life — in the near future as well as in the long term. So take a walk, hit the beach, ride a bike: whatever makes you feel relax and comfortable.

Once you do that and be in a comfortable position, you should be able to analyze, reflect, visualize, and dream.

This is the first step towards success.

2. Become an Optimist

As Oscar Wilde said:

"What seems to us as bitter trials are often blessings in disguise."

And yes, this may not be the truth each and every time, but you would like to think that it is, right?

Being an optimist gives you the much-needed confidence, comfort, and a feeling of joy that you always need. Liberate yourself from the negativity that is all around you, make sure you set aside every negative thought that tries to enter your mind, and try to find the positives in every situation. You will soon a completely different — a more positive — person in you.

There is always an opportunity in every setback and failure. You only need to be able to see it, pick yourself back up, and grab that opportunity. And you can only do it if you do not let yourself down for long. That's only possible with a positive frame of mind. Optimism is the only answer.

3. Rid Yourself of Excuses

We have already discussed the importance of accepting responsibility in chapter 5, but it is an important tip that is worth mentioning again.

It is human nature to give excuses. Nobody likes to say, "I was responsible for that".

But the key to unlocking your maximum potential is to be able to rid yourself of all possible excuses and accepting responsibility to whatever happens in your life.

You know what those excuses are? They are nothing more than the lies you tell yourself when you wonder why you are not reaching your true potential. Those excuses — those lies — are the only thing that stands between your current state and the position you actually deserve.

Once you get rid of excuses and start accepting the fact that whatever happens in your life is mostly because of the choices and decisions you made earlier, you will get on the right track.

The moment you realize that there is no one, who will magically come into your life, swipe a magic wand, and make your life ten times more awesome than it currently is, you start working for yourself. That is when you are able to see your true potential.

4. Don't Sell Yourself Short

You are beautiful; you are a lot more capable that what you think of yourself, and you are awesome!

Stop selling yourself short. If you do not realize your true potential, nobody else will. More often than not, it is not the excuses that stop us in our way, but it is our limited mentality and lack of belief in ourselves that does not allow us to succeed.

You are a lot more capable and talented than what you give yourself credit for. It is important to realize this so you can dream big, achieve bigger, and maximize your potential. But before you could maximize your potential, isn't it a prerequisite to first realize that you have more potential than you currently think?

This is why it is one of the most important tips you will read in this book. Believe in yourself and stop selling yourself short.

Do you know the success of the famous undefeated champion, Floyd Mayweather?

He understands his strengths, realizes his power and capability, and use them to win games and excel towards continuous success.

In his own words, "Do you think I gave up my whole life just to say there is someone better than me out there? Absolutely not!"

And while it may seem like ego and over-confidence, it is not. You see, it is important not to sell yourself short. If a champion — a professional fighter — starts believing that his opponent is better than him, he has lost the battle already. How could Floyd Mayweather defeat an opponent who he thinks is better than him? It is not possible.

Even if he could manage to defeat a fighter who he thought is better than him, Floyd's abilities or his confidence will not grow. He will always feel that he got lucky. He will not have any trust and confidence in his abilities, and it will never allow him to grow, improve, and unlock his maximum potential.

Floyd Mayweather has a killer instinct that you also need in your life to face difficult situations and overcome different challenges.

5. Start Learning

"There is no wealth like knowledge; no poverty like ignorance."

You want to be become the best version of yourself and more successful in your life? Start learning.

There could not be a better advice than this.

You see, we live in a modern age where information is updated on a daily basis. You can never relax, underestimating the dynamism of this world, feeling that you know everything. Nobody can know all the important things. This is why there is a learning process that goes on till the moment you die.

Or as Jim Rohn puts it in the following words, "All the information you need to succeed already exists. The only problem is that you are not exposing yourself to it."

Read as much as you can. As a matter of fact, my recommendation would be to set aside a specific amount of time on a daily basis, just for reading and learning new things. Learn something new every day and keep an open mind towards it.

It will just be a matter of months when you will be the smartest person in any room. After all, you will be everything a new thing almost every day.

6. Be Grateful

Good things do not happen to ungrateful people. And even if good things do happen to them, they won't be able to realize their importance or feel happy about it. Where's the fun in that?

Always be grateful for whatever it is you currently you have and whatever achievements you are going to accomplish in the future. Be thankful and humble about the life and privileges you have — even if you do not have a lot. It is an important step towards achieving better things.

According to Ralph Marston:

"What if you gave someone a gift, and they neglected to thank you for it. Would you be likely to give them another gift? Life is pretty much the same way. In order to attract more blessings that life has to offer, you must truly appreciate what you already have."

Isn't there a lesson for all of us?

7. Accept Change

Whether you like it or not, change is an important part of our lives. Everything changes. After all, we live in a very dynamic and fast-changing world.

So how can you achieve your maximum potential if you are not responsive and accepting of change?

It is very important to become more accepting, responsive, and adapting to change. For instance, when smartphones first came into the market, it was a major change over feature phones. The new smartphones, however, made our lives a lot easier. You can connect with the entire world, send messages to your friends and family members on the go, check emails, be in touch with your clientele, and do lots of other productive and business-related activities.

Now, what if you hadn't adapted to smartphones? Other people would still be using them, but you would be missing a lot of opportunities to grow and accomplish better things in a relatively shorter amount of time.

Change is inevitable. And more often than, it is important and necessary. Realize this, become more adapting to changes in your life, and you will soon feel liberated and a lot happier.

8. Plan Ahead and Focus on Long Term Planning

You cannot achieve bigger things without careful planning.

Once you know what it is that you want to achieve, things become a lot simpler and easier to understand.

Whenever you are distracted, you can ask yourself, "Do I really want to achieve that goal of mine?" Soon, you will be back to work.

Similarly, there will be times when you will procrastinate. This is when a person usually tries to do the less important tasks, instead of completing his primary objectives in accordance with his main goal.

But you can only realize that you are procrastinating if you know what your main plan is. If you do not know your primary goal, you will never be able to reach it.

Besides that, whenever you procrastinate and lean towards doing less important tasks, you can ask yourself, "Does doing this task help me to achieve my goal? Does this help me in accordance with the plan I set?"

You will get your answer. If it does not help you achieve your goal, you should not be doing it.

Apart from all that, planning ahead and having a long-term focus is always a good thing. In fact, for most famous and successful people, the long-term focus is the key to your success.

What do you think is the primary strategy of Warren Buffett? He says that his favorite holding period for an investment is "forever". He always has a long-term plan in place, and this is why he succeeds most of the time.

Even when the economy recently suffered a global depression, Warren Buffett did not suffer huge losses. He was one of the few people who still managed to stay afloat. Forecasting, long-term plans and persistent focus are some of his chief qualities that you should adopt.

Another example of Warren Buffet's long-term focus is that following his landmark decision to acquire the remaining shares of Burlington Northern Santa Fe Railroad; he did an interview. In that interview, he focused on his long-term attention and long-term plans, forecasting that railroads will still be essential 100 years from now.

9. Become Mentally Strong

If you want to become more successful in life, you will have to become mentally stronger than you currently are.

Life is tough, and you will often face difficult situations in life. How are you going to deal with those situations if you are not mentally strong? The key is to mold yourself in almost every aspect.

You need to improve your emotional endurance, as well as your strength against fear and mental barriers. Always remember that your lack of mental strength is often the #1 reason why you fail. Most people wrongly assume that it is your financial weakness, relationship problems, or lack of physical strength or stamina, but it is rarely true. It is all in the mind. After all, this is why this book is about creating a mindset to unlock your maximum potential.

If you believe you can, you are most likely to do it.

Let me give you an example.

The UFC Mixed Martial Arts is one of the most dangerous and intense sports in this world. It requires absolute strength and unprecedented physical capabilities that often seem beyond a normal person's reach. But even for MMA fighters, their mental strength is regarded as their more important weapon.

According to Randy Couture, the former UFC heavyweight, and lightweight champion:

"Although most fighters believe that the fight is 90 percent mental and 10 percent physical, they train 90 percent physical and only 10 percent mental. That is going to have to change as MMA continues to evolve, or those fighters will be left behind."

If mental strength is more important in the most physically demanding and intense fighting competition, then wouldn't it be important in your normal life, too?

This is where most people fail because they do not realize the importance of becoming mentally stronger. The moment a person becomes emotionally and mentally stronger, he can truly unlock his maximum potential.

10. Set Shorter Goals

Another important tip is to set several shorter goals,

instead of one long-term objective.

Yes, you want to be successful, but having only this does not get you anywhere. In order to help you achieve this goal and maximize your potential, you need help from several shorter and more achievable goals that you can easily follow.

Break down the steps you need to complete in order to achieve your one, main goal. Make sure you convert that one big objective into smaller achievable parts.

Breaking those steps down are not only easier to track your progress, but they also give you a definitive way to get started. For example, most bloggers plan for the next week. They do have a long-term objective, e.g., what they want to achieve next year or a year after that. But they also break their goals into smaller steps that only cover a week or so.

So by the end of a week, they can track their progress and see if they have been doing it right or not. If they are lagging behind, they can easily make small adjustments in either their daily routine or their weekly (shorter) goals to make sure they meet those objectives.

It is a lot easier to track, and it gives you a more

realistic view of how to achieve a big future objective.

11. Take Action

Nothing beats this tip.

Take action.

All the tips and techniques that you have read in this book will be of absolutely no use for you if you do not take the necessary steps.

In other words, you will never be able to achieve your maximum potential if you do not act! If you finish reading this book and get back to your current lifestyle, it is not going to help you at all. It won't change anything. And I'm sorry, but some of the things do need to change, don't they?

If you truly want to unlock your maximum potential and become the best version of yourself, you will have to take action. There will be a few sacrifices; there will also be a few compromises. But in the end, all will be worth it.

12. Become Your Own Competition

Before you finish reading this book, understand this

very important concept.

Become your own competition. This is probably one of the best lessons you can learn from this book.

As we have already discussed that people with a negative or fixed mindset become too obsessed with winning or not losing. They become so crazy of the concept of winning that they fail to realize what is their primary goal in life and how are they going to achieve their maximum potential. As a matter of fact, they end up being mediocre or — at best — the same as others and never reach the level where they could explore their best version and achieve their true potential.

The tip is to always become your own competition. Try to better yourself with every passing day. It becomes a never-ending — but a very healthy — competition. You start learning new things every day, and that is how you improve in your life.

Not competing with your own self can be really dangerous. You may end up winning a marathon, but you will still be not happy. Why? Because there will always be someone who won the "Ultimate Marathon" or the "Iron Race" and finished way ahead of you.

Does this mean that you failed?

It certainly does not mean that. You did great, and you should be proud of it. But that is only possible if you set your own benchmarks, compete with yourself, and stop obsessing about what others are doing in their lives.

You have to understand that every person is different from the other. Some people progress faster than others, but it does not mean that the slow learners are stupid. They would be excellent other ways.

According to Einstein, "Everybody is a genius. But if you judge a fish by its ability to climb a tree, it will live his whole life thinking that it is stupid."

The idea is to become your own competitor. Whenever you set out to do something important, your primary goal should be to improve and become better. Ultimately, you will be able to become the best possible version of yourself.

And you know what does that mean?

It means that you would have unlocked your maximum potential then.